Nightlights

Nightlights

Stories and Advice to Help Your Child Discover
Peace, Confidence, and Creativity

By David Fontana, PhD, and Anne Civardi

CHRONICLE BOOKS
SAN FRANCISCO

First published in the United States
in 2003 by Chronicle Books LLC.

Conceived, created, and designed
by Duncan Baird Publishers Ltd.

Library of Congress Cataloging-in-
Publication Data is available.

ISBN: 0-8118-3955-9

Typeset in Mrs Eaves
Printed in Singapore

Book Design: Dan Sturges
Cover Design: Ayako Akazawa
Commissioned Artwork: Fiona Hewitt

Distributed in Canada by
Raincoast Books
9050 Shaughnessy Street
Vancouver, B.C. V6P 6E5

10 9 8 7 6 5 4 3 2 1

Chronicle Books LLC
85 Second Street
San Francisco, CA 94105

www.chroniclebooks.com

Storytellers:

Joyce Dunbar

Kate Petty

Louisa Somerville

A NOTE ON GENDER
In sections of this book intended for parents,
to avoid burdening the reader repeatedly with
phrases such as "he or she", "he" and "she"
are used alternately, topic by topic, to refer
to your child or children.

C O N T E N T S

About this Book

This is a book of stories to read to children, but stories with a difference. It's a collection of twenty interactive meditation stories that have been specially written to calm and relax your child at bedtime, while at the same time engaging and stimulating his or her imagination.

These stories also help children in many other important ways. They help them to focus their minds and develop their powers of concentration and visualization, as well as learn more about emotions and feelings. Although not meditations in the strict sense, they do serve as a good preparation for learning real meditation later on.

Reading the stories aloud, you draw your child into wonderful adventures where he or she meets all sorts of inspiring and intriguing characters. By encouraging children to describe and elaborate on the illustrations that accompany each story, and then interact with the tale once it's under way, you can transport them into fascinating new worlds and help them tap into their boundless creativity. These new worlds may be, in various ways, exciting, but they are also reassuring — they are safe, happy places to spend a little time.

The stories are written to appeal to girls and boys from around four to eight years old. But individual children differ greatly in their speed of development, and you are the best judge of when to read them.

Each story opens in the same way — with your child closing his eyes, picking up his magic lantern and imagining himself walking down an Enchanted Path (into the realm of dreams) with the magic lantern to light the way.

At the end of each story there's a list of positive affirmations to help draw out the story's deeper meaning. These address issues such as shyness, separation and loneliness; gently help to instill qualities such as confidence, love, sharing, courage and patience; and encourage your child to explore and understand certain situations that may arise in his or her life. A "values and issues index" is given on pages 140–4.

There's a short stretching and relaxation exercise you can do together just before you read one of the stories: see pages 24–5. And at the back of the book (pages 132–9) are some breathing and visualization exercises that will help your child on the road toward true meditation.

It's best to read the introductory sections first (pages 8–25). They discuss the needs of children and how the stories can help these needs. The stories themselves are best read at bedtime, when your child can relax and enjoy them to the fullest. We hope you will share his or her enjoyment, and that reading the stories together further strengthens the bonds of love and understanding between you.

Helping Your Child *to* Grow

The experiences children go through are crucial in shaping the adults they will become. A happy childhood, filled with love, security and encouragement, as well as stimulation and excitement for the senses and the imagination, allow a child to develop self-esteem, self-confidence and a positive, optimistic attitude to life. These qualities will serve him well through the years that lie ahead. Children's enduring

A Child's World

For a small child, adventure lurks around every corner, behind every closed door, at the top of every stair. So the stories that appeal to young children must somehow combine this intimacy and this excitement. They must have echoes of the familiar, everyday world, yet at the same time they must open a pathway into the novelty of an enchanted kingdom.

Children also love being involved, and learn best through activity. The interactive way in which these stories are presented therefore has a special value. Be sure to take the chance to discuss together what part your child plays in the story, to describe and elaborate on the pictures, and to talk about all the fascinating new worlds and characters he or she is introduced to.

attitudes toward themselves and others, the strength and warmth of their relationships, their life goals and ambitions are all formulated largely by the way people behave toward them and by the opportunities and interests to which they are introduced. Nowhere is this more apparent than in the development of their intelligence and in the growth of their imagination and creativity.

Reading and being read to not only stimulate children's imaginations, but also help them to experience the full range of their own emotions. The stories in this book will by turns excite, enchant and thrill growing minds. Children are invited to become deeply engaged in unfamiliar situations — and in the process to experience themselves more fully, and discover more about their own strengths and vulnerabilities, their likes and dislikes, and in due course their ability to invent stories for themselves.

At the same time, they will learn about other people, about the many different kinds of relationships, and about the ways in which people communicate with each other and express themselves, as well as help and support each other.

The basic idea of this book is to introduce children to the magic not just of the written word but also of their own inner selves.

9

Imagination
and Creativity

Imagination and creativity, inextricably linked, enter into every aspect of life. All creative acts start in the imagination of their creator — to be creative, you must be imaginative. This means that you must learn to think up your own ideas and be flexible rather than conventional in your thinking. Psychologists describe this kind of thinking as *divergent* or *open-ended*, in that it opens up new possibilities instead of homing in on a single right answer.

We all have an innate need to be creative, and unless this need is satisfied from childhood onward, part of us will remain frustrated and unfulfilled.

There are few things that stimulate a child's imaginative and creative development more effectively than reading stories to them, and helping them to develop the reading habit for themselves as they grow. In an age dominated by visual media, such as films and television, stories have the advantage of reaching and enriching the child's inner world. Visual media leave little to the imagination. Stories, however, allow children to respond imaginatively. Their imaginations reach out to embody and embellish the cues provided by the storyteller. Inwardly, they visualize a scene in their own unique way. The storyteller provides a framework, which the child's imagination furnishes. There is evidence to suggest that children who are deprived of these important experiences may never develop their full imaginative potential later on in life. It is therefore essential that children are given stimulating opportunities for free and independent thinking. Stories, complemented by evocative illustration, provide such opportunities in abundance.

Stimulating Your Child's Imagination

Each story in this book begins with your child imagining herself in a particular environment or setting. This is designed to draw her into the "meditation", to think of herself as an integral part of the story, to stimulate her imagination. However, some children may find this imaginative projection more difficult than others.

You can help by first getting your child to relax and calm down before you begin to read (see pages 24–5). Then ask her to close her eyes and imagine the scene — say, the jungle in "The Joyful Jungle". If she cannot visualize it immediately or isn't quite sure what a jungle looks like, you may have to prompt her gently by saying something like, "It's a place that's full of big, tall green trees, plants, flowers, birds and animals. You can hear birds chirping and squawking loudly. You can see monkeys jumping from tree to tree." The more vividly you set the scene, the more you will stimulate her imagination and allow her to visualize the rest of the story.

Dealing *with* Anxieties

The stories in this book are designed to be calming, to take children into a secure, comfortable inner world. Things that might seem stressful in a real-life context — snakes in the jungle, or the prospect of performing in public, or even the next stage of growing up — are presented in such a way that anxiety is stripped away from them. Any fears that might be prompted at first are very soon resolved — that is, they are shown, in this context at least, to be groundless. The reassuring tone of the stories (which you can help to reinforce with a reassuring tone of voice) puts children's minds at ease and helps them shed the stresses of the day.

For children can experience stress just as much as adults. No matter how much we love our children and seek to give them freedom for self-expression, they are inevitably constrained by the prohibitions and regulations we impose on them for their physical safety and social education. Small children can find these constraints perplexing and frustrating, and become confused and unhappy at their own rebellious reactions to them. Once they have reached school age, the possibilities for stress are even greater: children can easily be troubled by apparent failure in class, by quarrels with friends, or by the hostility of older children. And what is greatly valued may, of

course, be lost: a best friend might move to a different school, or for various reasons a parent might not be around as much.

It's important therefore that children are helped to find a tranquil space within themselves where life's troubles fade into the background. In finding this space they come to appreciate that happiness arises not only from the way we are cherished and loved by others, but also from the way in which we can be at peace with ourselves. They will learn to turn to this space, to tune into this inner music, during anxious or unhappy times. Their best-loved stories will have a role in this – not merely as a refuge but as a source of strength, a collection of influences that have helped to shape a true sense of the self.

Moreover, the stories here have been written to instill important qualities in life. The fact that the child *enters the world* of the narrative, instead of being merely a spectator, helps her to identify with the fictional experiences. She comes to identify with certain emotions, and with the way in which certain kinds of difficulty can be met and overcome. She learns that, like the characters she meets, she, too, can overcome challenges, think independently, be caring, helpful, brave, generous, and find love and friendship in her relationships. For those interested to know which particular issues these stories subtly address, there is a values/issues index on pages 140–4.

Finding Identity
through Stories

From an early age, young children take readily to the idea of symbols, the idea that one thing can represent another. Watch a small child at play and notice how easily a piece of wood can become a sword, a cardboard box can become a house, an old sock a doll.

Likewise in stories, each character and each event can stand for something beyond itself. The best stories have universal implications, and say something meaningful and truthful about human qualities.

A child, involved in the stories, begins to absorb (through emotional identification) constructive rather than destructive ways of relating to the world, as well as (through imaginative visualization) creative patterns of thinking. The characters are designed to symbolize aspects of the child himself. By engaging with the story he explores his personal strengths and vulnerabilities, and his attitudes toward himself and the other important people in his life. Such exploration is important for his development. Young children are not born with a sense of who and what they are. Much of this knowledge comes from experience, and in particular from what adults tell them.

How Reading Boosts Confidence

The more children read, or are read to, the more new words they learn and the wider their vocabulary becomes. This is a great help when it comes to their schoolwork — particularly writing their own stories or speaking in front of others — and gives them confidence to use words that they might otherwise not have encountered.

Don't worry if you come across a word that your child doesn't recognize in any of the stories here. Quietly explain what it means and then carry on reading. At the end of the story you might wish to remind your child of any new words and ask if she can remember their meanings.

If children are told often enough that they are bad or foolish, or if they are exposed to constant failure and the embarrassment that goes with failure, they inevitably develop a poor self-image. Children flourish best in an environment of acceptance and encouragement, in homes where they are loved and where their hopes and fears are considered important, where adults spend time listening and talking to them, where their ideas and opinions are taken seriously.

Sharing the intimacy of these stories with your child reminds him that he is important enough to have your full attention, that his inner world is understood and accepted by you, and that he can have confidence in himself as a much-loved and valued person.

The Art *of* Reading *to* Children

Although the stories in this book are designed to be read at bedtime, their intention is to engage children rather than to send them to sleep. In this respect, your attitude and tone of voice as storyteller are all-important. You should feel that you are as fully *inside* the story as the child.

Unless you convey the impression of being alive to the narrative, believing in its unfolding perceptions and events without reservation, your meditative story will fail to have the desired effect. Adult and child should travel the story together. Many adults in fact report that they have re-discovered something of the wonder of their own childhood while reading to children. Show by your tone of voice, your speech rhythms and your facial expression that you share your child's reactions of surprise and excitement.

Routine is of great importance to small children. Having a regular time and place for storytelling – the bedroom at bedtime – encourages your child to give you immediate attention. It also helps to let her realize that storytelling adds bonus time to her waking day. Anything that postpones going to sleep usually ensures any child's complete cooperation!

You'll need to decide how often you want to read these very special stories: it's important that they don't become commonplace. Don't rush them. Allow the atmosphere to build up as you read, and pause frequently to allow your child to picture the scenes imaginatively, and to respond to the questions the stories pose. If she seems keen to talk about anything in the story once you have finished reading, encourage her to do so — in her own time and in her own words.

Holding a Child's Attention

Most young children find it hard to concentrate on one thing for long and are easily distracted. However, concentration is the basis of all meditation, so when telling the stories you need to be able to gain, and hold, their attention. It's a good idea to start with a simple relaxation and stretching exercise (see "A Way to Begin" on page 24), or either one or both of the breathing exercises (on pages 132–3). These will pre-empt any restlessness and help the child to expend any excess energy.

You know best how to speak to your child, according to age and level of understanding; but words such as, "Let's read a special kind of story tonight, one that helps you see all sorts of nice pictures in your mind," will usually be appropriate. Don't overtax the child with lengthy and unnecessary details before you've even started. Inner experience is just as real to children as outer experience, so the stories will usually speak for themselves.

Creating the Right Mood

After an exciting or tiring day children sometimes find it difficult to settle down and listen to a story. However, the interactive nature of the stories in this book should be a great help in teaching even a restless child that it's perfectly possible to be active in the mind while relaxing in the body. Establishing a routine of bedtime storytelling is also vital. Your child quickly comes to look forward to the intimate experience of settling down with your undivided attention. The idea is to create a safe and relaxing atmosphere.

Before reading a new story, you might wish to recall with your child the last one you enjoyed together. What happened in the story and why did it happen? Ask him what part he played in the adventure. What did he see and what did these things look like? What did they sound like, feel like, smell like? And how did he feel about what happened in the tale? Share with your child your own reactions to the story, while taking care not to dominate his own imaginative thinking. Prompt him if he leaves out something that you remember made a big impression on him at the time, but as always keep things light and non-judgmental. You can start on the new story once you have created the right atmosphere of pleasurable anticipation.

If you have more than one child, they can experience the stories together, so long as the age difference is not too great. But avoid any hint of competition. Each child must enjoy the experience in his own way. If, after listening to the older child's experiences, the younger one copies what has just been said, don't accuse him of repetition. Instead, gently ask him if he found anything else particularly interesting or enjoyable.

Activities for Daytime

Although the stories in this book will be used mainly at bedtime, they can also be read during the day if you feel that your child might be receptive to them at such times. Another daytime distraction, when your child is looking for outlets for her energy, might be to devise a few activities arising from the stories. You could suggest that she draws or paints one of the characters. Or she might like to enlist the help of a brother, sister or friend to act out a story.

Older children might enjoy writing stories using similar themes and ideas to those covered here. If so, they should concentrate on writing as clearly and vividly as possible. Some children also like to write short poems, while others might opt to dramatize the stories using their toys. All imaginative work of this kind assists the child to assimilate what she has learnt, as well as enhance her creativity. Older children might wish to read the stories for themselves, or read them out loud to you, and this also should be encouraged.

Talking *with* Your Child

The stories here encourage communication between you and your child. Talking with children in a way that they understand, though without talking down to them, is something of an art, and requires the adult to try to see the world through the child's eyes. The illustrations are intended to

Children's Language

Each child develops language at his or her own speed. Girls are often a little more forward than boys, perhaps because they're usually slightly less active physically. Some children start talking much later than others, then quickly catch up. Talking and reading to your child is the best way of encouraging language. From birth onward, talk to him about anything and everything. Describe what you're doing and why you're doing it, talk about the things you see in the house, or on your walks, the flowers in the garden, the things you watch together on television. Remember that most children have a much larger passive vocabulary (words understood) than active vocabulary (words used).

The descriptive and vibrant way in which the stories here are written encourages children to write their own stories in this way, using words they might otherwise not have thought of.

help this special kind of seeing, and also to facilitate the process of exploring together all aspects of the story — with appropriate questions from both sides.

Encourage her to describe what she sees in the pictures, and then invite her to think imaginatively about them. "Who do you think lives in that house?," "Where does that little path lead?," and so on.

Use similar methods with the stories themselves. "What?" and "Why?" questions are particularly good for stimulating a child's imagination. Draw her attention to important parts of the story that she may have missed. Show that you are puzzled by something in the story or in one of the pictures, so that the child sees that her answer is there to help your understanding, not to test her knowledge. Praise her responses by saying things like, "I love the way you described that ... ," or "I never thought of that myself ... ."

Encourage your child to improvise stories of her own. These can be based upon the pictures, or they can be developments of the stories, along the lines of, "What do you think happened next?", or "Who else do you think might have come into the story?" But, as always, never press the issue. Sometimes a child will feel like improvising, while at other times she may not want to. It's important to remember that creativity can never be forced.

Affirmations

As we think, so we are. If we view ourselves, our relationships and our lives positively and optimistically, in terms of success rather than failure, then we can literally transform our day-to-day experiences. It's even true to say that positive people are healthier in both mind and body. Negative thinking is a habit that many young children begin to pick up at an early age from the people and the world around them, so it's vital that they are taught to think positively as soon as they can. Of course, the best way to help your child to become a positive thinker is to be one yourself.

To accentuate the positive in children's lives, we have ended each story with a list of affirmations designed to help you draw out the story's deeper meanings — the attitudes, values and virtues that are subtly embodied in the narrative. Introduce these affirmations to your child with words such as, "Here are some of the things the story has been telling us" — avoid phrases like "teaching us", as you don't want to give the impression that the stories are lessons!

Once you have read the affirmations together, invite your child to add some of his own. Or you can ask him for these before you read out the affirmations from the book. In any discussion that follows, avoid asking direct questions such as, "Why do you think love is a good thing?" Instead, use indirect language — "I wonder why love is a good thing?" This makes it clear that you are pondering the matter yourself and that his ideas are of help to you (as are his comments on the story itself: see page 21). It's a great mistake to assume that children want us to know everything. Children delight in knowing more than we do, in doing things we can't do, and in believing that their thoughts are truly helpful to us. The self-confidence that accompanies this delight is essential to the development of their creative thinking.

Ending the Day on a Positive Note

The more relaxed your child is when she goes to bed, the more likely she is to enjoy trouble-free sleep. One way to help her do this is to share a quiet time with her before you read to her your bed-time story. You can discuss the good things that have happened in her day, as well as the prospects you are both looking forward to tomorrow. You could also talk about her achievements and praise her encouragingly for anything she has done especially well.

It's best not to bring up issues that might be worrying her, as this could prevent a good night's sleep. These problems, of course, shouldn't be dismissed, but should be discussed during the daytime. Any television she watches or any book she reads close to bedtime shouldn't be too gloomy or frightening. Instead use bedtime to give her a positive and happy view of life and the world around her.

A Way *to* Begin

B efore you start to read one of these stories, or any other bedtime story, you might like to do this short, simple stretching and relaxation exercise with your child. This could become a routine you can share together every night. Most children really enjoy this kind of quiet, gentle exercise, and it's a good way to get them to relax, calm down and burn off any excess energy at the end of a busy day. By helping your child to relax her body, you help her to relax her mind, too. This makes it easier for her to empty her mind of thoughts and concentrate on the story you are about to read.

First ask your child to lie on her bed, or on the floor with her head on a cushion. Ask her to put her hands on her tummy and imagine there's a balloon inside it. Now say to her:

"Close your eyes gently.
Breathe in slowly and deeply through your nose
and let the balloon inside your tummy slowly fill up.
Now breathe out as slowly as you can through your
nose and let the balloon become smaller and smaller until
there's no air left in your tummy at all."

Ask her to do four more breaths like this and then say:

"Now squeeze your hands up into a ball, as tight and small as
you can. Curl your toes as much as you can. Curl up your
knees to your head. Close all your body as tight as a flower
bud, so tight it seems it will never open.

"Now slowly, slowly, one petal at a time, unfold like a flower
and stretch. Stretch open your hands. Spread your fingers.
Make your fingers grow, grow, grow.
Look, your hands are like beautiful petals.

"Now drop your hands. Let them go. They are SO heavy.

"Relax your feet, until they are so heavy you can't lift them.
Imagine they're warm and toasty. Then imagine this lovely,
warm feeling moving up your legs and slowly filling your
whole body — your bottom, your tummy, your hands, your
arms, your neck and even your head.

"Now relax your mind. Is it ready to listen? To listen to the
story you're about to be told? I think it is!"

Angela's Toy Shop

Close your eyes and listen to your breathing, the air going in and out, keeping you alive. How much air can you breathe in? Can you breathe all the way down to your toes? If you can, you might fly. Just like thoughts. Thoughts can fly. Thoughts can take you anywhere, especially with the help of your magic lantern. Pick it up and stand in its circle of light. The circle gets bigger and bigger. Now walk down the Enchanted Path. Where will it lead you tonight?

Ah! You're standing outside a brightly lit window — a window that's full of toys! You peek in through the glass door. Inside is a small woman with fluffy blonde hair. Her name is Angela.

Angela's fast asleep in her chair because she's had such a busy day — lots of children visited her shop today. So many toys went off to new homes that she's spent the evening putting all kinds of new toys into their places on the shelves. A delicious smell of chocolate wafts over the room. It's the hot chocolate Angela drank before she dropped off to sleep.

You step inside. Angela doesn't see you. She's still fast asleep. You walk along the rows of toys, quiet as a mouse. There are the games and the craft kits, the puzzles and building bricks, the toy cars and the fancy dress outfits. There are the dolls and stuffed animals. And there's a beautiful, big, cuddly brown bear.

This is a special toy shop and these are special toys. In the spell of your magic lantern, you can hear what they're saying to each other …

"Isn't this the best place ever?" says the big brown bear enthusiastically.

"What happens now?" asks a small gray monkey, who seems a little nervous to you.

"We can't wait to be chosen," says the big brown bear, "because it's only when we're chosen that our real life begins."

"Why's that?" asks the small gray monkey, looking puzzled.

"Because children have a special magic," answers the bear. "As soon as they choose us and love us, they give life to us. Almost like giving breath. Then we play games and have adventures."

"What if we fall down?" asks the monkey.

"Then we get loved better, and get lots of cuddles," answers the big brown bear, smiling.

"What if we get lost?" asks the monkey.

"Then we get found," says the brown bear.

"And what if a new toy comes along, and we're not loved any more?" asks the monkey.

"That doesn't happen," says the bear. "Old toys are loved just the same. Look! Look over there."

And the brown bear points to a glass cabinet. Inside is a collection of very old toys. There's a prancing donkey who's lost his prance and a threadbare lion who's lost his roar. There's a kangaroo who's lost her hop but still has her baby in her pouch. And an old china doll who's lost one of her pink dancing shoes.

The old toys are talking, too. You take your magic lantern to the glass cabinet and slide open the door. What are they saying to each other?

"Those were the days," says the lion. "When we were all new and loved."

"Yes. And we're still loved," says the kangaroo. "That's why Angela keeps us here even though we're older now. What better place could there be?"

"Tomorrow the children will come," says the lion. "They'll admire us through the glass and wonder about our lives. We'll see their warm breath on the glass, and their fingerprints. Their eyes will shine. They'll smile and laugh when they see us. I like watching the children …"

" … and wondering about their lives," adds the kangaroo who's lost her hop.

Now take your magic lantern and walk among the shelves. Can you hear Angela breathing in her sleep? Perhaps she's dreaming about her toys. Soon she'll wake up. You look at the toys, shining the lantern in their faces. "Choose me! Choose me! Choose me!" they seem to be saying.

Which one will you choose? Maybe Angela will let you have one of the old toys from the glass cabinet? They're very precious, and the happy lives they have lived show on their faces. Or will you choose a bright new toy that's just been put up on the shelf — a toy with a bright new life to come?

Think of the most lovely toy in the world. Think what it looks like, how it feels. Is it a toy that you've had for a long time? Then you've given it your magic already. Now you can give it a hug. Or is it a toy you long for? If it is, keep a look-out, because one day you'll see that toy and you'll know it was meant just for you ...

 Affirmations

- Look after your toys and the love you carry for them in your heart will always be there to keep you company.
- You might worry about being left out when someone new comes along — like a new brother or sister. But parents love their children all the same. Just like Angela loved all the toys.
- Children have a special magic. In their imaginations toys come to life. Take care of your imagination. Let it glow.
- Love is a merry-go-round. The-more-you-give-the-more-you-get, the-more-you-give-the-more ...

Dancing with Butterflies

Close your eyes and think hard about a party. It's going to be the best party you've ever been to. What would it be like? Let's see if you can find out! Pick up your magic lantern and walk down the Enchanted Path. Where will it lead you tonight?

You're in a garden that's blooming with all different flowers. There are red ones and purple ones, yellow ones and orange ones, and tall ones with big blossoms that sway in the wind. Tiny insects dart from flower to flower, sucking up their sweet nectar.

Just then a movement on the far side of the garden catches your eye. You see a small creature sitting on the white garden gate. It's a caterpillar — not a big, hairy one, nor a small, spotty, yellow one, but a green one that looks quite ordinary to you. So you make your way across to the gate, over grass that tickles your toes.

"At last!" you hear the green caterpillar cry with joy, as she holds up and reads a white card with edges of gold. On it, in spidery writing, is written: "The Queen of the Butterflies invites you to attend the Butterfly Ball."

"Hurrah! Hurrah! The night of the party's arrived! I shall go as I am, of course," says the caterpillar with glee. "Brilliant green for a brilliant ball!" She does a little twirl, then stops, as she catches sight of you stepping toward her.

"Oh, but you must come, too. Yes do, yes do!" she laughs. "It'll be such a grand party." You look down at your clothes. How can you possibly go to the ball dressed as you are? You feel so disappointed.

"If only Isabella were able to come! But look," says the caterpillar, pointing to a little blob on a leaf, "she's still a chrysalis."

All of a sudden, the chrysalis starts to wiggle and jiggle — "pop, pop, pop" it goes. Struggling free, and panting a little, something is emerging, something with two beautiful big eyes, two long, thin antennae, six spindly legs and a short, slender body.

You watch as the creature stretches out gracefully. And, like magic, two magnificent pairs of wings start to unfold. It seems that what was once a blob has turned into the most beautiful butterfly!

The butterfly's wings are wet. She flaps them up and down slowly and they flutter in the wind until they are dry. The wings dazzle you, they are so beautiful. In them you see all the shades of the sky, of rainbows, of sunsets, and even of starry, moonlit nights.

"Oh, how lovely you look, Isabella!" gasps the caterpillar. "Hurrah! Hurrah! Now you can come with me to the Butterfly Ball."

Then, with the tip of one wing, the butterfly touches your head. All at once you begin to change, too. You've grown your own beautiful butterfly wings. How light they feel, so light you hardly know they're there at all.

Now it's time to try out your lovely new wings. So you follow the butterfly as she flies around the garden. Together you flutter from one flower to the next, and then you dart up into the sky.

Higher and higher you fly, heading toward the moon and the twinkling stars. Below, you watch as the garden becomes smaller and smaller, until it's no more than a tiny dot in your eye. Isn't it wonderful to fly like a butterfly, as light as a feather, dipping and diving, swooping and soaring, floating and gliding with the greatest of ease?

Now you hear music among the flowers below. It's soft, gentle music that sounds like the tinkle of sweet, tiny bells. You see strings of fairy lights stretching from one tree to the next. You hear laughter and singing. Then you see them! Thousands and thousands of them — a carnival of caterpillars, a bevy of beautiful butterflies, all gathered together for the Butterfly Ball.

There are big, graceful butterflies whose satiny wings shimmer in the moonlight. There are tiny butterflies with bright little wings that catch hold of the starlight. There are butterflies with wings that glimmer and glisten as they flutter to meet you. And there are caterpillars — big hairy caterpillars, small, spotty, yellow ones, and green ones that look quite ordinary to you.

"What magnificent wings!" they call out. How proud you feel. How happy you are to be at the ball.

And now it is time to enjoy the party. What will you do? Will you join in all the games? Will you feast at the banquet and drink cups of sweet nectar? Will you flutter your wings as you dance until dawn? And when it's time to go home and climb into bed, will you dream of the caterpillar — the one who invited you to the best party ever, the friendly green one who asked you to the Butterfly Ball?

Affirmations

- Be proud to be yourself and comfortable with your looks.
- Like people for what they are, not how they look.
- When you're feeling happy, share your happiness with others.
- Always make the best of everything! Even when you're disappointed, good things may come along soon.
- At a party you'll meet all sorts of different people. Join in with them, and enjoy their company as much as you can.

The Dream Makers

Close your eyes and try to imagine where your dreams come from. Do they just enter your mind, or does someone put them there while you're asleep? Let's see if you can find out! Pick up your magic lantern and walk down the Enchanted Path. Where will it lead you tonight?

You find yourself in the middle of a beautiful park. There's the new moon pale like the end of your fingernail, and the stars are twinkling high above you. All around you see trees, flowers and grass. On the lake there are swans, with long, slender necks in the shape of the letter S. What a lovely, peaceful place!

Suddenly, you hear someone laughing behind a bush, and you go to find out who's there. It's two tiny children, half your size. They're giggling a lot and they're trying to shovel what looks like glittering sand into their buckets. The trouble is, the sand

doesn't want to stay in the buckets. It keeps trying to escape! Everywhere are lots of tiny children trying to collect the glittery sand. What could this sand be? It can't be just ordinary sand, or they wouldn't be so careful not to spill any. So you ask your new friends what it is.

"Why, it's starshine," they tell you, "the stuff dreams are made of. We're Dream Makers. Every night we gather up starshine and put it into our Dream Machine to be turned into lovely dreams. Come with us and we'll show you."

The Dream Makers take you to a big, shiny, metal machine in the middle of the park. Now they empty their buckets into it, and the machine starts to shudder and shake, rattle and gurgle. Round the back, you can see the Chief Dream Maker working hard as he turns the big handle.

All at once out floats a batch of bright, shiny dreams, each one as light as a feather. They're floating off to have some fun with all the world's children while they sleep. You watch the Dream Makers jumping on to the dreams and riding them off high into the sky, past the pale moon and the twinkling stars.

But wait! There goes a dream all by itself! Quickly the Dream Makers try to catch it, but off it rockets — gone! "Oh dear," says one of them, sadly, "a nightmare's escaped."

Now your friends let you empty some starshine into the machine. Once again, it shudders and shakes, rattles and gurgles. Then out pops the most beautiful, shimmering dream you could ever imagine.

"This dream's just for you," says one of the children. "Hop on board and it'll take you wherever you wish." You thank them and promise to visit again.

Now it's time to leave the Dream Makers, so catch your extra-special dream and close your eyes. I wonder where it'll take you tonight …

Affirmations

- The world goes dark every night to give our eyes a rest.
- Dreams are the safest place to be — if you fall, you never hurt yourself.
- Even if you have a nightmare, remember you're still safe in your own cozy bed.
- The night is the time to sleep and dream, not to worry. Close your eyes, relax your mind, and dream.

The Singing Mountain Children

Close your eyes and imagine a castle. It's an old castle with a moat all around it. What would it be like to go inside that castle? Let's see if you can find out! Pick up your magic lantern and walk down the Enchanted Path. Where will it lead you tonight?

Up to a huge, heavy door decorated with a magnificent golden shield. You push against it with all your might. Slowly, very slowly, it creaks open and you step into the most enormous room you've ever seen. It has thick stone walls and big, high windows, each one as tall as a house. Hanging on the walls are gigantic flags, embroidered pictures and shiny suits of armour with crossed swords glinting in the sunlight. Look! Look up. There are birds flying high above you. It's such a massive room that the birds look tiny to you — just like swallows high in the sky. Perhaps they *are* swallows.

You're in the castle, back in the past, a long, long time ago. There are lots of people about, in strange old-fashioned clothes, like the clothes knights and princesses wear in picture books. You admire their beautiful robes and sparkling jewels.

The most important people here are the king and queen. There they sit on golden thrones, perched high on top of a platform. You watch as their servants bring them plates of fine food and glasses of wine.

At the end of the room, you notice a stage. A great crowd of people, some standing, some seated, are all looking in the direction of the stage, as if waiting for a show to start. Now you hear the sound of trumpets — a wonderful fanfare of trumpets. You realize what it is you're all there to see. It's a royal performance, especially for the king and queen.

One of the queen's pageboys comes up to you. Oh no, you think. Why couldn't he just leave me alone? But, smiling, he takes you by the hand and leads you to another throne, right next to the king and queen. As he sits down beside you, the pageboy chatters to you about the performance that everyone's waiting so eagerly to see. So by the time the show begins you know exactly who the performers are going to be.

They're the children from a farming village miles from the palace, high up in the mountains. Once a year they come down to the valley to put on a show for the king and queen. The mountain children make their own costumes decorated with eagles' feathers they find among the craggy cliffs. They sing songs about farm work — milking goats and shearing sheep — and what it's like to live in the mountains, up in the clouds, where the eagles fly.

As the children run on to the stage, everybody in the room claps their hands together loud and fast. You join in, too, clapping as hard as you can. How fantastic it is to be in a castle, sitting on your own purple, velvet throne, right next to the king and queen!

Everybody's just as excited as you. They seem to like these children from the mountains, even though their costumes are so ragged and their movements on stage are a little stiff. Some of them are nervous, but that's hardly surprising because, as everyone knows, even really famous singers can get a little scared before a performance.

After the applause has died down, the singing starts. First the children all sing together, very nicely you think. Then two sing together, then three, then four, and finally one little girl all by herself. You think she's very brave to sing all alone to so many important people. While she sings, someone plays a big brass horn, with a deep bellowing sound just like an elephant. A little boy squeezes an accordion that's much too big for him. It's not the best music you've ever heard — not like the trumpets. But nobody minds because everybody's enjoying themselves so much. And everybody knows that all the singers are trying their very best.

Now the queen leans over to where you're sitting. She invites you to go on to the stage and sing a song of your own. You feel very nervous. But everybody is

46

smiling and encouraging you to perform. So you step on to the stage and start to sing the song you like best. At first you sing quietly and then you get bolder. Soon you're singing at the top of your voice. Now you feel confident and brave.

The king and queen laugh and cheer at the end of your song. Can you imagine it? The king and queen laughing and cheering! And this particular king and queen enjoy all the singing so much that the tunes are still playing in their heads when they drift off to sleep that night … dreaming of goats, meadows, sheep and clouds, and eagles that shed their feathers on to a beautiful hillside far from home. And they dream of the sweet song you sang to them …

 Affirmations

- Remember, almost everybody gets a little nervous before they sing, perform or speak in front of other people.
- If you try something once, you'll find it easier the second time around. The more you do something, the better you get at it.
- A lot of kids are shy when they enter a room full of strangers. But if you join in with them, you'll soon start to have a good time.
- So long as you try your best, people will be proud of you – and you'll be proud of yourself!

As Gentle as an Elephant

Close your eyes and imagine yourself in a hot, hot place. It's so hot that the countryside has turned brown and dry from the heat of the burning sun. What would it be like to live somewhere like this? Let's see if you can find out! Pick up your magic lantern and walk down the Enchanted Path. Where will it lead you tonight?

You find yourself in the middle of a grassy plain — in Africa. Tall, dry grass, stretching toward the blue sky, is all around you. You see a tiny mouse scurrying about near your feet. She's looking for something to eat. As you watch, you feel yourself getting smaller and smaller, until you're as tiny as a mouse, too. Now the grass seems like a jungle of tall trees to you.

Soon you're hot and thirsty. You feel sweat dripping down your face, as you lie panting in the grass. Then you see what

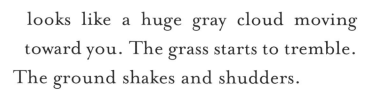

looks like a huge gray cloud moving toward you. The grass starts to tremble. The ground shakes and shudders.

The big cloud comes closer and closer, casting a shadow over where you're hiding. Now it's changing shape. You watch as it grows legs and a tiny tail. You see a head, with gigantic, flapping ears and a long, long nose that twists and turns. Can you guess what creature the cloud is really?

It's an elephant — one of the biggest animals in the world. The elephant looks as tall as a mountain to you. At first you're afraid. The elephant's so big and you're so little. But then you see that even though he's huge and heavy, he places each foot down gently, taking care not to crush any tiny animals that stray into his path.

Now the elephant stops. His big dark eyes look down at you kindly. Then he reaches out to you with his wrinkly trunk and beckons you to clamber up. Slowly and gently, he lifts you up high, then lowers you carefully on to the top of his broad, bristly back. You can just see out over the elephant's wide head as he carries you along, swaying slowly from side to side.

You feel safe, and you know that the tiniest creatures are safe too, as the elephant picks his way carefully past them.

Now the elephant brings you to a big pool of water. You slide down his trunk and splash the cool water all over your hot face. Then you take a long refreshing drink.

All around are other animals drinking heartily, too. You see zebras reaching out with their muzzles to guzzle the water. A giraffe bends down her long neck and takes a big sip. A hippo opens his mouth wide and lets out a deep grunt. What other animals can you see? What other noises can you hear?

Affirmations

- Let other people help you when things get difficult. They often know exactly what to do. Just like the elephant knew where to find water.
- Don't judge people by their size and weight. Big people can be just as kind and thoughtful as small people.
- It's important to stay calm in difficult or scary situations. Then you will have a clear head to work out what it's best to do next.
- Sometimes you might feel much smaller than others around you — but that doesn't mean you don't count as much as they do.

The Clown
in the Sky

Close your eyes and imagine a clown. He's the biggest, tallest, brightest clown you've ever seen in your life. What might this clown do — this clown who lives far, far away? What magical tricks might he perform? Let's see if you can find out! Pick up your magic lantern and walk down the Enchanted Path. Where will it lead you tonight?

Out beneath the night-time sky full of bright, twinkling stars. And look! Look up! Someone else is there, way, way above you, someone smiling and dancing. Slowly he spreads out his long arms, as wide as you can imagine, as he lights up the stars. Now he leaps high into the air, and the dark sky turns to the brightness of day. With a swoosh of his arms, it again turns to night. Watch his graceful dance. Night and day, night and day, with every dancing step that he takes.

Look at the clown's brilliant costume, shining and spangled with stars. Now he does a cartwheel. Round and round and round he twirls, too fast to follow. Now he stops and juggles the planets. See how he spins them like tops.

Listen! Can you hear the tune that he dances to? It's a long way away, far, far out in space. It's deeper than silence, stiller than stillness. It's the music of the planets as they move. It began before time. The clown sings to this tune, a song so sweet that the silence strains to listen. Out of the listening silence comes a listening star, a brand new star that twinkles and shines. It's come to join all the others, all the other bright stars.

He's a very special clown, this clown in the sky. He looks after the planets, he looks after the stars — the yellow, red and blue stars that light up the sky. He protects the hot sun and the silvery moon. He takes care of the comets that travel far, far out in space. He guards the meteors, those shooting stars that streak and fall through the sky. He keeps the whole universe tidy and clean so that every night it sparkles, twinkles and glows — just for you.

The clown likes watching the Earth. Sometimes it makes him smile. When the clown smiles, he spreads bright golden rays of light all around. But sometimes the Earth makes him sad, and he cries. Then his tears are like pearls, as big as moons but as light as balloons. Then shadows fall. Can you think of one thing that might make the clown sad? Can you think of one thing that might make him happy? The sadness and the joy fill his big heart. When he stretches out his long arms he hugs the whole universe.

This clown is bigger than the tallest giant. Bigger than Mount Everest, the tallest mountain on Earth. In fact he's bigger than the Earth itself. His reach is so wide, he can reach out into other worlds. If you were to pour all the lakes, all the rivers and all the seas of the Earth together into a cup, to him it would be no bigger than a thimble. Sometimes, just for a moment, he steps into other worlds, to show off his magic tricks.

Now he scoops up a handful of glittering stars and trickles them through his huge fingers.

Next, he catches a big meteor, pops it into his mouth and pulls it out of one ear.

See what an acrobat he is as he rides a black horse, on his feet, on his hands, on one hand. See the bear that dances and dances with him ... and then gives him a great big bearhug.

See the birds he pulls from his magic hat — silvery moonbirds, golden sunbirds, twinkling starbirds.

See the kite he flies and the rainbow-striped hoop that he spins. Feel his sigh, like a gentle breeze that floats in the air.

Watch out when he sneezes!

Hold tight when he hiccups!

But now he has something specially for you — a present, a surprise. You don't know what it is. Ah! He's sprinkling some new stars in the sky just for you. In your mind, join up those stars with the biggest crayon you can imagine. What shape do they make? Is it an animal — your special animal to do the dance of the sky with the clown. Or maybe it's something else. A spaceship, perhaps, that can take you all the way to the moon and back? Or is it a person, someone you love and care for?

And now the clown is tired, very tired. His movements are very slow. He takes off his black velvet cap with its bright orange trim. The night strokes his hair gently. Now he drifts quietly through the dark universe, carried by the hands of the night. Black velvet hands with long, smooth fingers. Star-shaped hands like yours, carrying the clown in the sky. Let him go now. Let him rest awhile. You can rest, too. And when you want to see him again, all you have to do is look, look up at the sky …

The clown will be there — always!

 Affirmations

- The universe is a very big place. But even the tiniest ant has a special place in it. As does the smallest child.
- If you ever feel a little afraid of the dark, think of the clown as he turns on the stars to light up the sky. Or sprinkles new stars in the sky just for you, to play with in your mind.
- Travel with your mind like the clown travels through the universe — it's amazing how far you can go.
- Wondering makes the mind grow wide. Let your mind go wondering all around the universe. The clown will look after you.
- Help the clown by keeping your own world tidy and clean, so it'll always be a lovely place to live in.

The Snow
Rabbit

Close your eyes and think about how warm you are, cuddled up in your own comfortable, cozy bed. What would it be like to live in a cold, cold place? Let's see if you can find out! Pick up your magic lantern and walk down the Enchanted Path. Where will it lead you tonight?

Big snowflakes are falling all around you. They glisten as they touch the ground. As you walk, the snow crunches beneath your boots. It should be cold, but you can't feel it because you're wrapped up so warm and dry.

Everything is still. But then a tiny movement in the snow ahead catches your eye. You wonder if you're mistaken, but no. Just over there, behind a bush covered with snow, a pair of dark eyes is peeking out. When you look harder, you see that above the eyes are two long, furry ears.

It's a large white rabbit, an Arctic rabbit. You're in the far North, the cold, icy North!

The rabbit seems to beckon you with a twitch of her long whiskers. Feeling very brave, you step toward the snowy bush, making deep foot-prints as you go. The rabbit sets off, using her big back legs to hop high over the soft, thick snow. It's almost as if she's saying, "Follow me, follow me," as she lollops along.

The whole landscape is frozen and still. Nothing is growing except for some tall, upright fir trees and some bare little bushes. You think that you and the rabbit must be the only living creatures for miles around. It seems as if the rabbit knows what you're thinking. She wants to show you some-thing. So you keep on following her, pushing your way through the snowy branches of the trees in the forest.

Now you arrive at a wide open space among the trees. There's a huge mound of snow right in the middle. The white rabbit stops and you stop too. Then she hops right

next to you. You stand quietly, wondering what this mound could be. Is something hidden inside? The rabbit sits so close that you're able to reach out your hand and touch her soft fur. She twitches her long whiskers again and something amazing happens. One whole side of the snowy mound shimmers and disappears. A big cave appears and you can see right inside.

There in front of you is a mother bear. She's a big white bear with two tiny newborn cubs. They're curled up together fast asleep, so cozy and warm. You keep very quiet — it wouldn't do to disturb a bear!

Now the rabbit hops softly on, and the snowy wall of the cave becomes solid once more. So you follow her as she bounds out over the ice and snow.

Here the world looks white and bleak and empty, but the rabbit seems to want to show you something more. She stops on a ridge and waits for you to join her. Then she twitches those long whiskers again and, like magic, the surface of the frozen ground in front of your feet melts away. Now you can see deep down under the ground! You see burrows and tunnels far beneath your feet where small furry animals dig about for insects and roots. They move very fast, stopping sometimes to listen before scuttling on. You wonder who they're listening for.

Then you see a bigger animal waiting silently in a side tunnel. It's a weasel looking for her lunch. Perhaps she'd like a juicy little animal to eat? The rabbit moves on, and you see that the underground world is covered in snow once again.

Now the rabbit leads you back to where you both started. She nibbles at the bark of the tree, before scrabbling with her paws for a bit of twig to gnaw on. "Poor, poor rabbit," you think. "When does she ever get enough to eat?" You stroke her gently. And once more she twitches those whiskers.

Suddenly, before your eyes, the snow melts and the ground is covered in grass. It's springtime! You can hear water trickling down from the rocks high above.

The place is alive with singing birds and all kinds of animals searching for food. Yellow poppies nod in the breeze. Your friend, the snow rabbit, wanders off to a juicy patch of grass. Then, with a flick of her tail, she disappears into the distance. You try to see where she's gone, but now you can only see her in your mind. Still … you know you'll never forget her.

Now it's time to snuggle up under your soft snowy covers, curled up and cozy like the two baby bears. In your mind you can follow the animals down the tunnels to their homes, or dance in the spring with the snow rabbit. Isn't it nice to know you're warm and safe, and you don't have to hunt for your food?

Affirmations

- Be aware of the insects and birds around you. Marvel at all the creatures that live their lives without you even seeing them.
- Even when things get tough, there are lots of good things to find.
- Remember how lucky you are to be warm and well fed — some people aren't so lucky.
- Enjoy the beauty of nature, even in the coldest winter.
- Be patient and good things will come your way.

Treasure under
the Sea

Close your eyes and imagine yourself sitting on the side of a boat that's afloat in the calm sea. As you look down below the rippling waves, your magic lantern catches hold of the moonlight. It shines like an Enchanted Path across the deep blue sea. Where will it lead you tonight?

You slip into the warm water and swim around like a fish, weaving in and out of your own stream of glistening bubbles. Then, like magic, the bubbles turn into two tiny seahorses, bobbing up and down in the water beside you. Now they dart forward and wait, dart forward and wait again. You're sure they want you to follow them. So after them you go!

A shoal of silver fish shimmers all around you, hundreds and thousands of them, tickling your skin. The seahorses swim along just ahead of you. It's as if they're guiding your way — past starfish glowing in underwater caves, past oysters whose pearls glisten like tiny moons.

Now you see the wonderful colours of the coral reef. The coral looks like a gigantic castle guarded by sea urchins. As you swim through the turrets and towers of coral, your eye catches something glinting deep down in the water. What is it, you wonder?

Full of excitement, you swim closer and closer. It's a treasure chest! The lid isn't quite closed and you see little pairs of eyes peeking out from the darkness inside. Slowly you lift the lid all the way back, and lots of funny little crabs scuttle out.

Then you see them — sparkly jewels and necklaces, bracelets and buckles. And a heap of shiny gold coins. One of the seahorses brushes his tail against a ruby ring. "Try it on," he seems to say to you. As the jewel sparkles on your finger, you wonder who it might have belonged to. A grand duke sailing over the ocean with his navy? Or maybe a princess, sailing to marry a prince in some faraway country?

The seahorses play with the jewels and shiny coins. "Go on, take some treasure," they seem to say.

Maybe just one thing, you think. After all, who would miss one little coin after so many years? But the coin isn't yours. Better to put it back, you decide, and leave it hidden here under the sea. Maybe someone else will enjoy finding it another day.

Now it's time to go. You say goodbye to the seahorses and rise through the water in a spray of bubbles. As you break out of the water, you see the rising sun reflected in the sea. It looks like a shining disk, just like the golden coin you held in your hand.

Even though the coin isn't there any more, you still remember it in your mind. You know it'll always be there to remind you of the treasure chest and the beautiful world you saw deep down under the sea.

Affirmations

- You can get pleasure out of something beautiful without having to own it. You can remember lovely things and enjoy them in your mind.
- You'll be happiest if you don't let friends or anybody else persuade you to do something you shouldn't — something you think might be wrong.
- If you really don't know what's right or what's wrong, try to let your feelings decide for you.
- Be sure never to take anything that isn't yours, even if you think the owner won't miss it.

The Statue
in the Park

Close your eyes and imagine yourself in a park. But wait! It's an overgrown park, all higgledy-piggledy, that nobody seems to look after. Do you think anyone plays in this park? Let's see if you can find out! Pick up your magic lantern and walk down the Enchanted Path. Where will it lead you tonight?

The moon is shining brightly and the stars twinkle above you. You see lots of messy, twisted ivy trailing over the crumbling walls around the park. Shabby-looking plants grow in between the broken paving stones, and the lake is all dirty and brown. At the end of the path you see a statue. You wander over to it.

The statue is of a woman dressed in old-fashioned clothes. She's wearing a long dress and a big stone hat tied under her chin. In one hand she's holding a flat garden basket. The stone that she's carved from has turned brown from the weather and there's moss

growing all over it. Written below the statue it says: *VIOLET DICKINSON : GARDEN DESIGNER : 1810 - 1895.*

The woman's face has a kind expression, and as you gaze at it she seems to smile at you. You look, then you look again. To your amazement, her eyes start to blink and her cheeks slowly change from stone to rosy pink. One by one, her fingers start to move, then her arms, then her legs. The statue's coming to life! Her stone dress is melting into real clothes. Now she lifts up her hat — it's straw, not stone any more! — and brushes off the moss. She looks down at you and smiles again.

"Hello," she says, "My name's Violet. What's yours?" Then down she jumps. "I don't suppose you'd help me tonight, would you? I've a big job to do."

That sounds like hard work, you think. Maybe you could just walk around the park instead.

"Oh, I understand," Violet says. "You probably just want to go and play."

You look at her face — she looks so disappointed. Perhaps it wouldn't be so bad to help her after all.

So together you walk down the path to an old garden hut. "Wait here," says Violet, as she steps inside. A moment later she appears again carrying a big bag

of garden tools. She leads you on through an archway covered in sweet-smelling roses to a part of the park you've not seen before. Here the garden is neat and tidy.

"I love this park," says Violet. "It's my home and I want to make it as beautiful as it was when I was a child. So I work hard on it every night. This is what I've managed to do so far. But there's much more to be done. Come, let me show you."

Together you return to the tumbledown part of the park. Here Violet unpacks her tools. There are tools for digging, for weeding and planting, for trimming and cutting. To your surprise, there are cans of paint and some paintbrushes as well!

Soon Violet is digging up weeds, cutting back the overgrown paths and turning over the soil with her large garden fork. You help by fetching the tools she needs and putting the ones she's finished with back in her bag. Some of them have become quite dirty but, as soon as you drop them back into the bag, they look shiny and new once again.

Now Violet opens a packet of seeds. Together you kneel down and scatter them over the soil. As each seed lands, it quickly grows into a plant with green leaves and a bud that opens into the most beautiful flower. In an instant the ground is full of joyful blooms.

Next, Violet walks over to the dirty, brown lake. She takes a bottle out of her bag, opens the lid and squirts silvery liquid into the water. With a gush and a gurgle, the water starts to bubble. Then it turns a clear blue. A family of ducks swim out of the reeds and splash about happily in the clean water.

Now Violet leads you to the playground, where the rides are all broken and rusty. Violet asks you to fetch a swing from the hut. But how will you lift it? Won't it be too heavy for you to carry? But no, when you find it, it's as light as a feather.

By the time you return, all the playground equipment looks shiny and new. You help Violet to put the new swing in the middle. Then together you stand back and admire the new playground. It's the best playground you've ever seen in your life.

"The children will love playing here!" says Violet, as the sky begins to turn light, and night turns to day. She hurries back to the hut, her work done. Climbing back on to her stone plinth she looks around her happily.

"How lovely it looks!" she says proudly.

Now she's changing back into stone. Her face, legs and hands stiffen and she's a statue once more. You take a last look at the work you've done together. Then you tiptoe quietly out of the park. Perhaps you'll come back one day to see Violet and to play on the brilliant new swing in the playground?

Affirmations

- It might take a while for you to complete a task, but it will be worth it in the end — so don't give up too soon.
- When you choose to help somebody, you might think it will be boring, or even hard work. But it often turns out to be fun.
- If everybody takes care of nature, the world will be a much better place for you and other people to live in.
- Making something beautiful or special for other people to enjoy makes you feel good, too.

The Weather
Dance

Close your eyes and imagine it's raining. Or is it hot and sunny? Perhaps it's snowing, or maybe a big wind is blowing? Think about all the different noises the weather makes. There's the soft, gentle pitter-patter of the rain, the whistling of the wind, the silence of falling snow. Now pick up your magic lantern and walk down the Enchanted Path. Where will it lead you tonight?

To a gray and gloomy garden that's still and quiet. There's no wind blowing. No birds are singing. No leaves are fluttering on the ground. There's no light and shade. You try to work out what's wrong with the place. The weather seems to have forgotten it altogether. That's it, you realize! This garden has no weather at all. How can such a thing be? How can you get out of here? It's so dull, it's making you feel drowsy.

Then, as if out of nowhere, a bubble appears and

bursts just over your head, sprinkling you with its moisture. Now your arms and legs feel very light, and your toes start to tingle. You look down. Your toes have silver rings and your toenails are silver, too. In this dull and gloomy garden, you want to dance … but where's the music? Listen. What can you hear? Drip … drop … drip … drop … pitter … patter … pitter … patter … It's the music of falling rain. You can feel it in your toes. You tiptoe around, tip … tap … tip … You lick the rain. You feel the rain on your skin. You're not just dancing with the rain. You *are* the rain and the rain is you.

The garden glistens and sparkles. You dance faster as the rain keeps falling … splish … splash … splosh … You're running and gurgling, bubbling and streaming, tumbling and falling, until you're gasping and laughing and out of breath.

You lie down and look up at the sky. How wintry and cold it looks. You stretch out your arms, and they stretch so wide. You stretch your legs and they feel a mile long. Your breath hangs like a white cloud above you. Around you, the garden is white. The trees are all fringed with frost, hanging with icicles. You don't feel the cold. You *are* the cold and the cold is you.

Slowly, you get to your feet. And the garden dissolves. You're on a huge, shining lake that's covered with thick ice. You glide along with long, slow movements. You know just what to do. But where did you learn? You didn't know you could skate like this. Fast as the wind you move, forward, round, then backward. Now you do a figure of eight, now you're spinning on your toes. You arch your back and look up at the sky. A snowflake lands on your face.

Out of the pearl gray sky, big snowflakes are dancing down all around you. So now you do your snow dance ... so gentle, silent, drifting. You're as light and soft as a feather. You fall on the rooftops. You fall on the trees. You fall on the mountains. You fall in faraway places where no one's ever been before. You fall by the polar bear's den and past the huddle of penguins. You fall on the frozen seas and on the albatross's wings. He flies with you, up toward the sun. Nearer, nearer, nearer, the sun changing from

 pink to red, melting the snow.

Down you dance again, a speck in a sunbeam. So now you dance the sun dance. It's the lightest of dances, dappling the woodland, kissing the flowers, ripening the apples that grow in the orchard. You shimmer and shine. You glint and dazzle. And then, as you rise higher and higher, you beam and burn. You are the throb, throb, throb of the heat in the desert. The lizard lifts his toes, because the sand is too hot to bear. The snake hides down in his hole. The spider scuttles. But you don't feel the heat. Only the light. You are the sun and the sun is you.

Now a silence. Then you start to grumble. Now a clap of thunder. You stamp in the skies. You bang on the clouds. You zig-zag through the blackness. Loudly you roar. Fiercely you flash. But when the storm breaks, you're out of the storm. When the rain pours, you've done with the rain. Now is the dance of the rainbow.

And so, in a long, slow arch — red, orange, yellow, green, blue, indigo and violet — you're the rainbow.

You reach so wide, with your hands in the skies, your feet in a mystery. You're everywhere and nowhere, visiting a place where no one can ever go. You are the dance and the dance is you.

But you've danced enough for tonight. Another night you can dance the whirlwind dance, you can dance the hurricane or the tornado. Or you can do the dance of a sunny summer's day.

But wait! What's become of the garden — that dull and gloomy garden? It was a place that you sometimes find in your mind. What have you done with it? You've danced it away.

Affirmations

- Enjoy whatever nature brings you — there's fun in the rainiest day, just as there's fun in the sunniest afternoon.
- People are very much like the weather in their moods. Everyone has dull days and bright days, stormy days and peaceful days.
- In your mind, you can become anything you imagine, even the weather. You can be falling snow or rain, or a great blustering wind, or even a tiny speck in a sunbeam.
- Dancing can make you feel happy. You can dance your troubles away.

Strangers in the Forest

Close your eyes and imagine your friends. Isn't it great to have such nice friends? What would it be like to make some new friends — maybe some children who are very different from you? Let's see if you can find out! Pick up your magic lantern and walk down the Enchanted Path. Where will it lead you tonight?

You're in a clearing in the middle of a forest. Running beside you is a bright little stream, all gurgles and smiles. All around you are trees, their leaves swaying in the breeze. You hear birds singing, each song sweeter than the last. It must be springtime.

You sit on a fallen log by the stream and listen to all the wonderful sounds. You're very happy to be here. Suddenly you hear a loud shout echoing in the forest. Someone, somewhere is calling out a word over and over again. Can you make out what this voice is saying?

"Fawn, Fawn," it seems to shout out. But that's the name of a baby deer and they're shy, gentle creatures, you think. Surely they'd be frightened by this noise.

"Fawn! Fawn!" the voice calls out again. You peer into the trees but you can't see anybody. Who could it be? It sounds like a boy's voice. Then you hear another word shouted, from another direction. This time it's a girl's voice.

"Fortune! Fortune!" the girl yells. Fortune? Do you know what that means? It means good luck. That's a funny word to hear shouted in the forest.

Now you hear the first voice call again, "Fawn, where are you?" and then the second shout, "I'm over here, Fortune!" This time they sound much closer together. Oh, they're *names*, you realize! Fortune and Fawn. What unusual names!

Just then you catch sight of a boy and a girl running toward each other among the trees. They seem very pleased to see each other and they're talking fast, as if they have lots to say and not enough time to say it all.

Then, to your amazement, you hear your own name called out, by both voices together.

Yours is just an ordinary name, not something unusual like Fawn or Fortune. But how do these two children know you?

"Oh, there you are! We've been looking for you for ages," says the girl, the one called Fawn. Smiling, she holds out her hand for you to shake and says hello.

You mumble something, instead of saying "Hello" loud and clear. After all, these children are strangers, and you're not sure you should be speaking to them at all. They look very unusual, too. The boy's dressed all in blue with what looks like a yellow bandage wrapped around his head, covering his hair. The girl's dressed in green and wearing a red headscarf. She has a big red spot painted on the back of each hand.

"Don't be shy," says the boy. "We couldn't wait to meet you. My name's Fortune. And this is my friend Fawn."

But still you're not sure. Who are these kids, you're thinking, and why does Fawn have those big red spots on her hands?

"Oh, you're wondering about the circles," says Fawn, seeing you look at them. "They have a special meaning. They show that I believe there's a spirit inside all people, animals and plants, which makes them live and grow. I'm called Fawn because where I come from people are named after the animal their mother dreams about the night before she has a baby."

"And where I come from, we're named after a good quality. I bring good luck," says Fortune proudly. "My brother's called Justice and my sister's called Friendly."

All this is a lot to take in. You're quiet for a moment as you sit and think about what Fawn and Fortune have told you. Then, because they seem so nice and somehow seem to know you, you start telling them about yourself — where you live, your family, your friends, your pets, and where you go to school.

Just then, to your surprise, out of nowhere and as if by magic, you see a big basket floating down the stream toward you, with a plain white cloth peeking over the edges. You watch as Fortune leans forward and plucks the basket from the water on to the bank of the stream.

"You see, I do bring good luck, don't I?" he giggles, taking some delicious food out of the basket.

And so you sit on the white cloth with Fawn and Fortune and help yourself to the tasty feast. You chatter and laugh together, not feeling shy any more. It's as if you've always known them.

And tonight, as you lie in bed, you think about how two children who are so very different from you in some ways are also very similar in other ways. And how pleased you are that they've chosen you to be their friend … Fawn and Fortune and you …

 Affirmations

- Throughout your life you'll make new friends. How lucky you'll be to have so many, all so very different from each other.
- Try not to judge people by how they look, how they talk or how they dress. Inside they're probably thinking similar thoughts to yours.
- It doesn't matter if you sometimes feel shy, but the more you talk to people, the bolder you'll get.
- Learning about how other people live makes you understand them more easily.

The Magic Pebble

Close your eyes and think of a mountain. It's the highest mountain you've ever seen. What would it be like to stand on the very top? Let's see if you can find out! Pick up your magic lantern and walk down the Enchanted Path. Where will it lead you tonight?

Look! There's a narrow, stony trail that winds its way through tall trees glistening with dew. Beyond the treetops you can see the peak of the mountain towering above you. The mountain looks beautiful and grand. It shimmers in the morning sun. You want to climb it. But you're not sure how you'll do it.

But wait! Someone is standing on the path in front of you. Perhaps he knows how to get to the top? His legs are skinny and his bare feet look rough and scarred from walking in the mountains. You gaze into his face. His skin is wrinkled like old leather, but his soft, green eyes look at you kindly.

"I'm the Mountain Man and I'll guide you," he says gently. "The mountain looks high but you can reach the top if you try." He asks you to follow him.

At first the path is level and you walk on easily. But soon it becomes steeper, then even steeper. It's hard to keep up with the Mountain Man.

Now you feel hot and out of breath. Sweat trickles down your face and your legs feel heavy, very heavy. The top of the mountain seems a long way away. How will you ever make it?

The Mountain Man stops and takes a big, round pebble from his pocket and puts it into your hand. "It's a magic pebble," he explains. "Whenever you think you can't get to the top, hold it tightly and believe that you can."

You continue along the steep path, following the course of a gurgling stream. There are stepping stones across the stream. You watch as the Mountain Man skips lightly from stone to stone, but you're too afraid to follow. The stones are slippery and far apart and you think you'll fall into the icy water.

"Remember the pebble," calls out the Mountain Man from the far side of the stream.

Tightly you hold the pebble. Suddenly you feel a burst of energy and you aren't afraid any more. You feel brave and confident as you leap from stone to stone across the rushing water. Soon you're near the top of the mountain, above the trees. On hands and knees you climb, pulling yourself up over giant boulders. Just when you feel too exhausted to carry on, you squeeze the pebble once more. And all at once, you feel the cool breeze on your face. You've reached the top! You're on the roof of the world. You've conquered the mountain. Look! Look at that view! Far, far below you, what can you see?

 Affirmations

- To succeed at something, you must first believe you can do it.
- Doing something difficult is like following a mountain path. It may become harder the higher you go, but you'll get there in the end.
- Reaching the top is worth all the struggle it takes. It makes you feel good about yourself, and you'll feel proud that you've done it.
- You may be afraid of things you haven't done before, but if you try them, you'll often find they're not as frightening as you thought.
- Learning to do difficult things with somebody else makes it easier for you to do them again, all on your own.

The Fireside Cat

Close your eyes and imagine a cat. It's a really big cat. How do you think this cat's feeling? Let's see if you can find out! Pick up your magic lantern and walk down the Enchanted Path. Where will it lead you tonight?

Down a long corridor to a cozy room in an old wooden house. A log fire's burning in the big stone fireplace straight ahead. It's a beautiful fire, with leaping orange and blue flames above and red glowing embers below. Sparks that look like tiny stars float up the chimney. You can smell the sweet scent of the apple wood that burns in the fire.

There's a deep armchair by the fireside. It looks so comfortable that you just have to curl up in it. As you settle down, you hear a loud rumbling purr coming from another armchair on the other side of the fireplace. It belongs to a big orange and brown stripy cat.

You think that the cat must be very lonely and bored sitting here all by herself.

"No, no," says a soft, husky voice, and you realize the big stripy cat is talking to you. She seems to know just what you're thinking. "I enjoy playing with other cats, but sometimes I like to be alone, to look in the fire. What do you see in there?"

When you don't answer, she adds thoughtfully, "Sometimes I see fat, juicy mice scampering across the carpet. And sometimes it's a kitchen table piled high with meat and cheese and fish."

Now you look deep into the fire to see what you can find for yourself. And there, among the flickering red and blue flames, you see a handsome sailing ship in a storm being tossed about in towering waves that tumble and curl. But then the logs shift and settle, and instead of the sea you're looking at a fabulous city with golden spires and carved stone buildings. Small birds fly between the window ledges and dart down to the sparkling fountains below.

"I see seas and cities," you tell the cat.

"Keep looking," she says. "What else can you see?"

As the logs burn down, the fire glows more and more brightly. Now you see fantastic creatures and caves, forests and lakes and tall snowy mountains.

"I see all the wonderful things in the world in the fire," you say. "And in the middle, where it glows like a heart, it's so peaceful, just like it is in this room."

"Ah," purrs the cat. And you're not quite sure if she's still talking — or just purring.

The fire shifts once again. A shower of shimmering stars drift up the chimney. What do you see now? Is it your favourite seaside place? A party? A room full of toys? It's up to you. You choose.

Affirmations

- It's important to have a special place where you can think and be calm, and where you can enjoy being by yourself.
- You don't have to feel lonely just because you're all by yourself.
  You can take time to explore your imagination. The more you use it, the bigger and better it gets.
- If ever you feel bored, all you need to do is read a good book.

An Ancient
Oak Tree

Close your eyes and breathe deeply, in and out, in and out. Listen to the sighing, whispering sound you make as you breathe out. It's a sound like the wind whistling through the leaves of a tree. Now pick up your magic lantern and walk down the Enchanted Path. Where will it lead you tonight?

The whispering grows louder and you find yourself at the bottom of a huge old oak tree. But the leaves that are blowing in the wind aren't on the tree. They're on the ground all around you, dry and brown, swishing back and forth, dancing and tumbling. Standing there, with the tree all bare, you start to wish it was spring and not the beginning of winter.

The tree is ancient — it's more than five hundred years old. As it sways gently in the wind, you listen carefully. Yes, it really does seem to be whispering to you.

"Look at the beautiful shapes of my branches," it murmurs. "Look at the lovely lacy patterns my twigs make against the sky." You sit back against the great knobbly tree trunk, and feel safe and happy.

Now you open your eyes. Everything has changed. The tree's covered in bright leaves. Birds flutter in the branches, the sun glimmers everywhere, making quick-moving shadows all around you. Now the world seems so bright and busy, you almost long for the thick greenery of summer to come and shade you from the dazzling sun. Again, the tree seems to whisper to you: "Look at all the new life in my branches — the leaves unfurling and the birds' eggs hatching."

All that activity begins to make you feel tired and your eyelids start to droop. When you open your eyes again, you're in cool, green shade. Everything is green. But as soon as you start to wish for more colours, the old tree is whispering to you once again. "Feel how peaceful it is. Now there's nothing to do but sit back and wait for the seeds to ripen." The warmth of the summer sun makes you fall fast asleep.

Now the wind's blowing through the leaves once

more. This time it whistles and howls. Wide awake, you think at first that the tree's on fire! It's ablaze with colours — red and gold and copper — and rocking like a ship in a storm. Ripe acorns drop at your feet. You pick one up and look at it closely. It could be a tiny golden egg in an eggcup. You don't need the tree to tell you how lovely it is now — you can see for yourself. But again you hear the whispering.

"Every season is wonderful," it says. "Enjoy each one. Take the acorn and plant it. Be patient, because it will take many springs and summers, autumns and winters to become a tall tree like me."

Now, in your mind, plant the acorn. Do you think your tree will live for five hundred years?

 Affirmations

- Look for the best in what's around you, now. There will usually be something to please you. Don't always wish for something different from what you have.
- If you're patient, you'll notice incredible changes in nature happening very slowly.
- If you plant a seed now, you're making something for the future.
- There's a saying, "Age brings wisdom," which means that the older you grow, the wiser you become!

Peter's Last Voyage

Close your eyes and think about a best friend, someone you've enjoyed being with and talking to most. What would it feel like if that person set off all alone on an adventure? Let's see if you can find out! Pick up your magic lantern and walk down the Enchanted Path. Where will it lead you tonight?

You're strolling down a sandy track toward a long wooden jetty that stretches out over the sea. There's a strong breeze coming off the water. It makes the wires of the sails go "ping" against the masts of the bobbing boats. The wind ruffles your hair. You can smell the salty water and the seaweed washed up on the beach.

You like it here — in the wind and the sun — and you're happy because you're on your way to visit Peter, the old sailor who takes visitors on trips around the island in the bay. Peter's your friend, and he lets you sit for hours with your legs dangling over the jetty while he works and tells you stories of his days at sea. There's always something for him to do — painting the boat, oiling the engine, mending the sails for the days when there's plenty of wind. Sometimes he lets you come down into the cabin where you can help him clean up the kitchen, or polish the brass handles until they shine. At other times you sit together on the wharf and see how many crabs you can catch with worms on a string, before throwing them back into the water. Peter's wife Queenie usually arrives just when you're hungry and thirsty, with a picnic of sandwiches and fruit and something to drink.

On really quiet days, when there aren't enough tourists to fill the boat, Peter takes you along, too. It's wonderful on board as you head out to sea. There are seals bobbing about near the island and seabirds wheeling around their nests high up in the cliffs. Those days are the best of all.

The tourist season is nearly over and you're hoping that today will be one of those special days — perhaps a bit of polishing, and sandwiches and a trip out to sea. You never know!

You see Peter and run toward him. He looks up from what he's doing and waves to you. As you get closer, you see that he's carefully repainting the boat's name, QUEENIE, in gold. It looks beautiful. In fact, the whole boat is looking very fine indeed. The sails are rolled up ready to be hoisted, and a little flag flutters at the top of the mast.

"Watch out for wet paint!" calls Peter. You sit down on the jetty and look around you. Something's different. Normally Peter stops what he's doing for a few minutes when you arrive, but today he seems much busier than usual. Queenie pops her head up from the cabin and offers you a drink — before you've even done any work!

Then Queenie says something that makes sense of all this activity. "He's finally off," she tells you. "Off on that voyage he's always promised himself."

You remember how Peter has often spoken of his last voyage, how he wants to go beyond the bay, across the sea to the warm south. How he wants to see whales and dolphins again, to speed along with the flying fish. Just one last adventure.

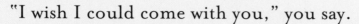

"I wish I could come with you," you say.

Peter laughs and shakes his head. "I'm afraid this is my adventure," he says, "just mine and nobody else's. Even Queenie's staying behind."

You can't imagine the sea and the jetty without Peter. How will you spend your days now?

"We'll miss him, won't we?" says Queenie. "But that means you and I can get to know each other better. I'll keep myself busy, because then the time will go more quickly. I've a map on the wall, so we can follow Peter's journey. I've got books, too, about the places he's going to visit, so we can find out about them while he's away."

"But why don't you ask him to take you with him?" you say.

"Because there are some things you have to do on your own," she replies. "And I'll be with him in a way, won't I, Peter? Both of us will be."

"You'll *always* be with me," agrees Peter. "Always in my heart."

"I'll wave him off proudly," says Queenie, "and you must do the same, because you have to be brave to go off alone. It wouldn't be fair to make Peter feel bad about leaving us behind. That would spoil his big adventure."

Soon the boat is ready. Peter comes over to you and gives you a hug. "Keep me in your thoughts," he says, smiling. "And I'll keep you in mine."

You wave him goodbye, and then slowly walk back down the jetty. You might not be able to talk to Peter for a while, but you'll be able to pass on his stories and even teach someone else how to catch crabs with a worm on a string. And you'll be able to visit Queenie. Peter will be having his adventure and one day you'll have yours, too, won't you?

Affirmations

- When you love people, you sometimes have to let them do the things they want to do, even if it's without you.
- Losing someone or something is often the start of finding other people or other things.
- Sharing stories about the people you love keeps them alive in your mind and in your heart.
- Friendship and love can stay strong even after someone has left you.
- You might feel sad when you say goodbye to someone who's going far away. But, if they're happy, you should feel happy for them.

The Circus of Dreams

Close your eyes and think about what you want to be when you grow up. What would it be like to be a doctor, a detective, an artist, or even a circus acrobat? Let's see if you can find out! Pick up your magic lantern and walk down the Enchanted Path. Where will it lead you tonight?

To a dark and dusty room. It's so dark that it takes you some time before you can see anything clearly. Then you see that there are clothes racks all around, bulging with costumes, and drawers overflowing.

A fat little dog wearing a green velvet jacket and a silver top hat greets you. "Ruff, ruff!" he says. "What will you wear for the party? What do you want to be?"

"What party?" you ask.

"The dream party, of course," replies the dog. He takes out a costume. "How about being an explorer? Then you can discover new lands and new cities."

"Not me," you say, "I'm not brave enough."

"Bless my whiskers!" says the dog. "Whoever heard of such a thing? This is where your dreams come true. Put on this costume and you'll have all the courage you need. And a map. And a compass. And … No …? Then how about this? A perfect magician's outfit. With all the tricks you can ever imagine."

"No, thank you very much," you say. "I don't know any tricks."

"In the costume is all the magic you need," says the dog. He goes on, pulling out each of the costumes in turn. "See, here's a doctor's costume. What? You're not clever enough? Put on this white coat and you'll be clever. You'll learn how to cure people when they're ill. What else do you say? Not wise enough? Put on this teacher's hat and you'll be wise. Not bold enough? Not talented enough? Not good enough? Not anything enough?" barks the little dog, scratching his ears. "Why do you think you're here? This is your Circus of Dreams. Here, you become whatever you wear!"

"And what are you?" you ask.

"I'm the dream dog," says the fat little creature

proudly, and he waggles his tail from side to side to show just how proud he is.

"Now, see here! With this dragon suit you can breathe real fire. With this space suit you can walk on the moon. With this diver's suit you can dive down into the deep blue sea."

"But, but ..." you say, trying to interrupt. "I'm not BIG enough!"

"Tickle my ears!" barks the dog. "Of course you're big enough. Put on any of these costumes and you grow to fit it."

You look along the row of clothes. "Have you got a ... um, um, um?" you splutter, because you can't see what you're looking for. You're not even sure exactly what it *is* you're looking for.

"How about this?" says the dog, holding out a sparkling costume with glittering gold leggings and a shimmering top. "This is a circus acrobat's costume. Go on, try it for size." So you slip on the costume and it fits just right.

Now you find yourself on a tiny platform high up at the top of a huge circus tent. You're caught in a bright beam of light.

Below is a circle of excited faces all looking up at you. The crowd are watching and waiting for you to perform. You feel no fear. You smile and wave. Then, toward you from a platform opposite comes a bar swinging on two strong wires. It's a trapeze.

Without thinking you catch hold of the bar. Your feet leave the platform. Now you soar through the air, letting go of your trapeze only to catch hold of another. Now you're swinging back again, this time holding on to the bar with only your strong feet and toes. Forward you go and backward, making the crowd below nothing more than a blur. You're spinning, twirling, dancing in the air. You feel light and free as a bird. With a spin and a somersault you land back on the platform. Your trapeze act is over.

Now you step on to the high wire. You look down for a second, then you look straight ahead. Carefully, very carefully, you feel your way with your toes. In your hand you hold four big bright rings. You begin to juggle them. At the same time, you make your way along the wire, looking only straight ahead. Whoops! A sudden wobble. One of the rings falls out of your hand. There's a gasp from the crowd below. But

you're not afraid. You smile as the ring turns into an exquisite white bird. It's all part of your act, part of the thrill, part of the danger.

You recover your balance and carry on walking along the high wire until you reach the opposite platform. There, taking a bow with you is the fat little dog. He winks. All at once you're back where you started, surrounded by costumes. You hand back your outfit.

"You'll come again, won't you?" asks the dog.

You know that you will. But which costume will you try next time?

Affirmations

- Never tell yourself that you can't be what you'd like to be. If someone else has done it, why not believe that you can, too?
- Life is full of possibilities. But you'll probably find that you're better at doing some things than others. Ask yourself what it is you're best at, then enjoy doing it well.
- When there's something worthwhile you really want to achieve, it's up to you to work at it — you'll be surprised how well you can do.
- Sometimes ordinary things are best. It's better to be a brilliant cook than a bad president! You don't have to dream of being someone unusual.
- Never feel that you're not good enough to be somebody special — you already are!

A Blackbird Sings

Close your eyes and listen — listen carefully. A blackbird is singing on a clear summer's evening. She trills and flutes like a magical piper. It's as if she's asking you into her garden. What would it be like if you accepted the invitation? Let's see if you can find out! Pick up your magic lantern and walk down the Enchanted Path. Where will it lead you tonight?

Outside you can hear the buzz of a lawnmower and the splash of a hose as someone waters her flowers. Somewhere else people are having a barbecue. The smells are smoky and delicious. You can hear these people chatter and clink their glasses together, but the blackbird's song is louder than any other sound.

You find the singing blackbird in a wonderful green glade that's surrounded by trees. A stream runs across one corner, tinkling over the stones as it flows. A gentle breeze sighs through the leaves.

The blackbird leads you to a basket that's sitting on the grass. She cocks her head and gazes at you with her dazzling black eyes. It seems that she wants you to look in the basket.

Inside there are lots of musical pipes. You pick one out and blow it, and you find that you can play a beautiful melody, just like that. You hop and skip all over the grass as you play the notes — up and down the scales, slow and dreamy, quick and rhythmic, loud and bold, soft and gentle. The trees seem to bend and sway as they listen to your beautiful music.

Now your tune comes to an end and you bow to your imaginary audience. What a performance! What a brilliant player you are! You put your pipe back in the basket and sit on the soft grass. As you listen, the blackbird starts to sing her sweet song once again.

But now it's as if the gurgling stream and the swaying trees are singing along too. Other birds join in — there's the coo of a pigeon and the hoot of an owl. Another bird whistles loudly. Their music sounds like a tune you've known all your life even though you're hearing it for the first time. And you know there's something you can add to it.

Now you reach down into the basket for the longest pipe. It's the one with the deepest notes. Again you start to play, low notes this time. You're part of a wonderful band with the blackbird singing, the tinkling stream like a harp, the trees swishing like cymbals, and all the other birds joining in like clarinets and trumpets and violins, and you're the pipe player. You're all playing together, listening to each other, one lovely melody after another.

The song is over. There's silence, but the final chords hang in the air and in your mind. Hold them there. Perhaps you'll still remember the tunes in the morning. Then you can sing them to your friends.

 Affirmations

- Nature is all around you, wherever you go. Be aware of all the birds, animals and plants around you — and look after them if you can.
- It's amazing what you can hear once you start to listen — but to listen well you need to be quiet for a while.
- Playing alone and being a star performer are wonderful, but playing with other people can be just as satisfying.
- The sounds of nature are like music all around you — a gentle, comforting music that never stops.

Like a Firefly

Close your eyes and think hard about the people who love you — all the people who can't be with you right now. What might they be doing tonight? Let's see if you can find out! Pick up your magic lantern and walk down the Enchanted Path. Where will it lead you tonight?

You're outside, running up a hill. You puff and pant as you climb higher and higher. It's dark, but you can see patches of light not too far away. These are the glowing windows of your school friends in their bedrooms — sleeping and dreaming, just like you.

Now you're at the top of the hill. You can see lights twinkling far away — so many, dancing like fireflies. As you watch, you become lighter and lighter, brighter and brighter. You feel just like a firefly yourself, flickering with light, darting from place to place! That square of light over there!

That's where your best friend lives! What do you think is going on behind that window? Is your best friend listening to a story just like you? Send some happy thoughts to your friend and — who knows? — perhaps your friend will send some happy thoughts back!

Now you soar even higher into the night sky. In another town a light is shining from an open doorway, lighting up the garden outside. It's someone else you love. Who is it? Look! Someone is standing there right now, outside the house, looking out into the dark night. A dog and cat are sitting there, too. Reach out and touch the dog's soft head. Feel his furry ear under your hand.

Fly, fly on. Now you're going to travel even further than a firefly can fly. You're going to travel all around the world and back again. Imagine, on this dark night, seeing the whole Earth below you. Big cities are lit up like birthday cakes. Smaller towns are little yellow dots. All the towns and cities are joined by strings of fairy lights that are roads and railways.

Follow one of these strings of light to the other side of the world. You might have to cross those great pools of darkness, without any lights at all. That's where the oceans are. But the world is turning, and over there it's getting light. Down there is a town in another country. Imagine what the kids there are doing. Perhaps they're just waking up. Imagine them opening their eyes. Maybe they've been dreaming about someone just like you.

Now come back to your country. Come back to your town, your house, your room, where it's warm and cozy, where someone who loves you very much is sitting beside you — right now.

Affirmations

- There are people who love you and think about you even if you don't know they're doing it. Even if they're far, far away. People don't forget you just because they don't see you every day.
- If you send people your happy thoughts, you'll be surprised how many good wishes you get in return.
- The world's a very big place, full of wonderful sights and fascinating people. Whenever you have the chance to travel, enjoy it to the fullest.

The Joyful Jungle

Close your eyes and imagine a hot, steamy jungle. What would it be like to walk through that jungle? What animals might you see? What sounds might you hear? Let's see if you can find out! Pick up your magic lantern and walk down the Enchanted Path. Where will it take you tonight?

It's dark. Slowly you feel your way along a twisty path that's overgrown with thick creepers. Rays of sunlight glint from high above and you can just make out the shapes of tall tree trunks. Big, wet shiny leaves, dripping with water, touch your shoulders as you step carefully forward. You're feeling a bit scared. Ugh! What's in those trees?

But just then a friendly face appears right in front of you — a happy face with big eyes and a big wide grin. Oh, look! It's a monkey, a small furry monkey, swinging by his long tail from the branch of a tree.

Quick as a flash, he somersaults down and lands lightly beside you. Standing in a sunbeam, his soft brown fur looks dusted with gold. Then, to your astonishment, he speaks.

"Welcome to our jungle," says the monkey. "Don't be afraid," he adds, seeing the worried look on your face. "This is a special place. Come! Let me show you." You take hold of the monkey's hand. His hairy arm tickles your skin as he leads you on.

Now a sudden flash makes you look up. High above you is a parrot, a magnificent parrot with feathers of red, blue and green. You watch as she flies toward a rainbow that spreads high across the sky. Now the parrot flies down, down, down, clutching a slice of rainbow in her beak. Flapping her wings excitedly, she presents it to a dull, brown bird sitting all alone in a tree. The bird squawks with delight as her feathers change from dull brown to red, orange, yellow, green, blue, indigo and violet.

"Parrot knows how to make other birds happy," says the monkey, grinning. "She shares all her favourite colours with them."

Now a movement in the bushes catches your attention. A pair of green eyes shine out like lamps in the dark. It's a jaguar, the fiercest hunter in the jungle! His spotty coat ripples as he prowls through the trees to meet you. "Grr!" growls the jaguar.

"Oh, don't worry!" says the monkey. "He's just showing off. The other monkeys and I used to be very frightened of him and then one day we just stood up to him. Now he realizes he isn't as strong as all of us together. I bet he'd even let you stroke his tummy."

And with that, the jaguar rolls on to his back, just like a kitten ready to play! Slowly, cautiously, you reach down to stroke his warm fur. His loud purr sounds just like a rumble of thunder.

You walk on with the monkey through the thick jungle. Now he stops and points down as a line of ants march across your path! You crouch down to look at them. They're hard at work, passing pieces of leaf, from one ant to the next, as far as your eyes can see. As they work, they sing songs and tell jokes to each other.

"These ants used to fight all the time," says the

monkey. "But now they have fun and work much better together." He grabs hold of your hand and off you go once again.

Next you spot a snake hanging from the branch of a tree. He sways silently backward and then he sways forward. And look! There's another snake, and another. There are spotty snakes, stripy ones, black, blue and yellow ones — all swaying together in perfect harmony.

"They're doing the snake dance," says the monkey, clapping his hands with joy. "Every day they work on their moves. And then they give us a show!"

The snakes sway faster, faster and faster. So do you, and the monkey does, too. Faster and faster you both twirl … until you fall dizzy and laughing on the soft jungle floor. You lie there exhausted.

When you get up, the evening chorus is just beginning. The jungle is alive with noises — whoops and whirrs, hoots and toots, whistles and shrieks. Now the monkey scratches and yawns. "It's nearly bedtime," he says. "We'd better make our nests. Follow me." And with that, he leaps on to a branch high above you. You climb up behind him. Up and up you scramble, higher and higher. Sometimes all you can see is your friend's long tail dangling in front of you. At last, you reach the top, where the monkey is already busy grabbing branches to make his nest. But how will you make yours?

"Here, I'll help you," says the monkey kindly. And together you make a nest of branches, leaves and twigs. It doesn't look very comfortable, but to your surprise, when you climb inside, it feels soft and snug. The monkey climbs into his nest. He reaches up with his hand and snuffs out the stars. "Night, night!" he whispers. But you're already asleep.

Affirmations

- Situations that might appear a bit frightening at first often turn out to be fun, if you let them.
- Working on something together is more fun and makes you feel better than fighting over it.
- Let others help you with the things you find really hard to do by yourself.
- Allow others to have their fun without spoiling it for them — even if their idea of fun isn't the same as yours.
- If you're very good at something, it's nice to share it with other people — especially your friends.

The River
Moves On

Close your eyes and imagine a river. It's a silvery, playful river that winds its way gracefully through the countryside. What would it be like to take a ride down this river? Let's see if you can find out! Pick up your magic lantern and walk down the Enchanted Path. Where will it lead you tonight?

You're lying in a little boat that's floating down the river. The boat rocks gently as it moves. The bright sunlight makes your eyes blink. All around you can hear the buzzing of the bees, the singing of the birds, the whistling of the wind, and the bubbling, gurgling water. Such gentle, calm and peaceful sounds.

Wonderful things come in and out of view — a darting dragonfly, a floating, fluffy dandelion seed, a leaping frog. You put out your hand to touch them but they come and go so quickly. Sometimes you feel a little frightened. But only for a moment. Mostly, you feel safe and happy. You like it here. You want to stay forever. But the river moves on.

Now the river goes faster. You manage to sit up to see more of the view. Now you reach out to touch things that grow along the riverbank. As you do this, the boat wobbles a little. You stroke the tall, fluffy reeds and the long, silky grass. You dabble your fingers in the rippling water. You feel the soft petals of a flower. You want to explore everything you can reach. Then everything out of reach. You stand up as carefully as you can. The boat rocks from side to side, and again you feel a little afraid. But you're so excited by the sights and the sounds of the river that you soon forget your fear. You like it here. You want to stay forever. But the river moves on.

Now you're standing up in the boat. It seems to find its way down the river, all by itself. You try to work out who's steering it. Here, the river life becomes even more interesting. A duck comes over to investigate. A swan guides her baby cygnets out of the way.

Then a sleek, velvety animal with big soft eyes pops her head out of the water, just for a moment, to take a good look at you — it's an otter. Now she dives away again. More and more things come into view. You like it here. You want to stay forever. But the river moves on.

Then, you notice that the water's beginning to move faster. It feels dangerous but exciting. Now, it rushes over the rapids. The boat rocks and spins in the swirling water. You're hurried along. Faster, faster goes the boat. You hold on tight, you breathe deeply, your heart beats fast. Now you're in a whirling pool where bright silver fish jump all around you. It's thrilling! It's amazing! You like it here. You want to take charge of things for yourself so that you can stay here forever. But the river moves on.

Now, for some reason, the boat glides very slowly. There's no current to move it

along, no sail to catch the wind. You're bored by this part of the river. You find a pair of oars hidden in the front of the boat and try to row yourself forward. It's very hard work. You don't feel you're getting anywhere. You don't like it here. You're worried you might be stuck here forever. You think about jumping into the river and swimming for the bank. But just as you're about to take a leap, the river moves you on.

Now you're on the wide open water. The boat no longer goes by itself. You're in charge! As you row, you see lots of other small boats, with other people in them. The boats seem to be doing a strange dance, weaving in and out of each other, and sometimes bumping into each other. Whoops! You fall overboard into the cool water! But straightaway many hands reach out and help you back into your boat.

You know that if you fall in again you can scramble back all by yourself. You know that you're able to guide your own

boat. You look at the water that stretches far into the distance in front of you. It looks full of fun, excitement and wonder. You take a deep breath. It won't all be easy. Sometimes you may hit rough water, or a storm, or a waterfall, or even a whirlpool. You may capsize, you may find a hole in your boat, or you may find yourself rushing toward the rapids, almost out of control. At other times the gentlest of breezes will carry you to the loveliest of places. Who knows? Perhaps you'll find a beautiful blue pool where you want to stay forever. But the river always moves on.

 Affirmations

- Life is like a river — it changes all the time. Sometimes you can take charge of the changes, but at other times there's nothing you can do — you just have to accept whatever is happening.
- Sometimes it's best not to do things that seem scary. But if you always turn down the chance to do something new, you'll miss out on all kinds of interesting and exciting adventures.
- Often we do things because other people are doing them — but sometimes it's better to go your own way.
- It's good to learn to do some things on your own, and not to rely on other people always doing them with you.

Toward True Meditation

The twenty stories in this book are not "meditations" in the strict sense. However, they do prepare a child well for true meditation. The benefits from this practice, both psychological and physical, include tranquility, improvements in memory and in bodily well-being, as well as the development of remarkable powers of concentration.

The key to meditating successfully, no matter which method you use, is concentration. You take a point of focus, such as breathing, and concentrate on it silently, returning to it each time the mind wanders away. With practice, attention wanders less and less, until eventually you experience the mind in its own pure state, like a clear pond when the mud settles to the bottom.

On pages 132-3 you'll find two short, simple breathing exercises to do with your child. Then on pages 134-9 you'll find some visualizations. These, too, help to focus the mind, as well as encouraging calm, creativity and self-knowledge.

As well as doing the visualization exercises together, you can play your own visualization games with your child. To start with you could ask her to close her eyes and picture familiar objects such as a beloved toy, or a familiar person. When she's older, she can visualize something more extensive, such as a walk to the park or visit to the seaside. If, with your help, your child can develop these powers at a very early age, she'll be better equipped to use visualization as a way to enhance personal performance as she grows. It's only a small step from here to visualizing herself remaining calm before she performs on stage, or when she's teased by classmates or admonished by a teacher. Under the guidance of psychologists, athletes now help to prepare for big events by visualizing themselves winning their race or clearing the high-jump bar. Physical healing is also known to be accelerated when people visualize themselves as being well. Visualizing yourself as calm and confident before taking an exam or speaking in public can work wonders for your performance.

Introducing your child to meditation is one of the most important ways in which you can help her to cope better with her life, both at home and at school. It can give even very young children power over their thinking and their emotions, help them to understand and accept themselves, and lead toward greater happiness. The breathing and visualization exercises on the following pages are the first step toward this true meditation. Along with the twenty stories, they will absorb your child's interest, lengthen her attention span, enhance her ability to concentrate, and start to build the self-confidence that goes with this ability.

Breathing *and* Concentration

With these breathing exercises, and in the visualizations that follow on from these, it's important that your child doesn't feel impatient or worried if he loses his concentration. Tell him that as soon as his attention starts to wander, he should thank his mind for telling him so, and then calmly return to the exercise.

Keep all the exercises short and light-hearted. Don't insist on them if your child seems uninterested.

Watching the Breath

Before you begin, ask your child to sit on a chair or on a cushion on the floor with his legs crossed, his back and spine straight, his head upright and his eyes cast downward. Ask him to gently pull back his shoulders, close his eyes and link his fingers together lightly in his lap. Now encourage him to become aware of his breathing: he should breathe deeply from his tummy (as on page 24). Ask him to put his index finger lightly on the tip of his nose, and then say to him:

"Breathe slowly through your nose.

Feel the cool air as it enters your nose.

Now breathe out slowly through your nose.

Feel the warm air leaving your nose."

If he puts too much effort into his breathing or exaggerates it too much, gently remind him to breathe normally. It's a good idea to demonstrate how to do this yourself.

Ask him to do five breaths like this.

Now ask him to sit as quietly as he can with his eyes still closed, while you count up to five under your breath. After finishing the count of five, say: "When you're ready, you can open your eyes." This is his first "sitting" meditation.

Counting the Breath

In this exercise your child is encouraged to breathe in through the nose slowly while you count to three, four or five, and then breathe out through the nose to the count of three, four or five. At first, he may find it a little difficult, but with practice he should soon get the hang of it. It helps if you count out loud, as rhythmically as you can, and not too fast or slow, like this:

"In, two, three, four, five.

Out, two, three, four, five."

Again, it's best if you can demonstrate this yourself so that your child can understand what he's being asked to do.

As soon as he feels confident counting his breath in this way, ask him to do three complete rounds. Then ask him to sit quietly with his eyes closed while you count to five under your breath; then to open his eyes when he's ready.

Helping Your Child
to Visualize

It takes practice before you can visualize anything you want — to conjure up an image in your mind. Children may find it especially difficult to relax themselves sufficiently and concentrate enough to empty their minds and visualize a particular object or scene. This step-by-step guide is a good way to start them on the art of visualization.

Step 1

The first step is to get your child to relax by doing either one or both of the breathing exercises on pages 132-3. While doing this, she should sit in a relaxed but upright position with her eyes gently closed.

Step 2

Now, to free her mind of any thoughts, speak softly as you give her the following instructions:

"Imagine a place inside your head, just above the top of your nose and between your eyes. Imagine there's a big, white screen in this special place. Now imagine that you can see any picture that comes into your mind on this screen."

Step 3

Now ask your child to concentrate on the blank screen and think of something from one of the twenty stories — perhaps the beautiful butterfly in "Dancing with Butterflies". Ask her to imagine this butterfly as you describe it. For example:

"It's a big butterfly with shimmering blue wings.

There's a big pink spot on each wing."

Then develop your visualization with a series of simple instructions, like this:

Step 4

"Imagine this butterfly as it flies in the air. It lands on a big red flower with a soft yellow middle. Now the butterfly sticks out its long tongue and sucks up the flower's sweet nectar."

Step 5

"Now imagine the butterfly leaving the big red flower and flying high into the air. Watch as it flies above the treetops toward the clouds. Now it's gone. You can't see it any more."

Step 6

"Let the butterfly fade right out of your mind.

Now the screen between your eyes is empty.

It's time to focus on the peaceful, comforting, empty space the butterfly has left behind."

A Flower Grows

Before you start this visualization, ask your child to curl up into a little ball on the floor, as tight as he can. Then explain that, as you talk him through the words, he should stretch up as far as he can reach, and finally, as the visualization comes to a close, curl back into a little ball on the floor again. Gently speak these words, with long pauses:

"Imagine you're a tiny seed in the ground, covered with soft, brown earth. You feel all warm and cozy as you listen to the pitter-patter of the rain that's gently falling on the earth above you. Now you feel the warm sun as it shines down on the earth. You start to grow … slowly, very slowly, until you are a little green bud poking up through the ground. You grow up, up, up. As you grow, your leaves begin to open, one at a time, until your long stem is covered in big green leaves. Now you feel the warmth of the sun as it smiles down on you and you open up into a beautiful flower with big yellow petals. You stretch up, up, up as tall as you can and try to reach the sun. The day is almost over and the sun disappears below the horizon. Slowly, very slowly, you begin to curl up into a ball until you are a tiny little seed once again."

By the Seaside

If your child is faced with a particular anxiety, it often helps to visualize a special place, somewhere she can imagine going to enjoy its calming atmosphere. Many children choose the seaside, so this is a good visualization to help them relax before they go to sleep. You might say something like:

"You're at the seaside, standing quietly on the beach. You feel the grains of soft, white sand between your toes, tickling them as you wiggle them up and down. The sun is high up in the cloudless sky. Now you walk toward the blue, blue sea. You can hear the waves as they roll on to the beach, one after the other. You can smell the salty seawater and the seaweed that has been washed up on the sand. You watch some funny little crabs scuttle sideways across the sand and then disappear into their holes. Far, far out at sea, you notice a beautiful boat sailing gracefully through the water, its big white sails billowing out in the wind. You can hear the sound of seagulls as they fly up into the sky and over the tall cliffs that rise high above the beach. You like it here beside the sea. It makes you feel happy, with the warm sun on your back, the wind in your hair, listening to the waves and the birds. Yes, this is a happy, peaceful place to be."

A Taste *of* Lemon

For this visualization exercise, which is particularly good for concentration and imagination, you'll need a lemon. The idea is for your child to experience everything she can about the lemon without actually touching it. Once again, she should sit in a relaxed but upright position, while you say something like this:

"Look carefully at the lemon in front of you. Look at its shape. Is it round or is it oval? What shape do *you* think it is? Now look at its appearance. Is it a bright yellow or a light yellow? Is it the same all over? What does the skin look like? What texture does it have? Is it bumpy or smooth? Is it shiny or dull? Now close your eyes and without touching the lemon imagine what it would be like to hold it in your hand and squeeze it. Is it hard or soft? Now imagine you're cutting the lemon in half. The two halves fall apart and you can see drops of lemon juice dripping out. You raise one half to your nose and smell that sharp, lemony smell. Now you bite into it and taste that sharp, sour taste. Did your mouth water? I bet you it did — almost every-one's does. But it was all in your mind. Your imagination, all by itself, was able to make your mouth water!"

A Special Person

This visualization gives young children the chance to imagine someone they love and get comfort from — a person with whom they feel relaxed, safe and happy. This is what you might say:

"Imagine a doorway. Now open the door — it's quite safe if you do. As you step through the door, you find yourself in a long corridor. At the end of the corridor, you can see a bright light shining . Look, look all around you. What can you see? What does the corridor look like? How do you feel? It's quite safe here but you can turn back any time you want. Now you walk down the corridor. When you reach the end, you see someone coming toward you. It's a person you love — someone who makes you feel very safe and warm. Now this person stands in front of you, smiles and says something to you. What does this person say? Now the person walks backward away from you, still smiling. You walk back down the corridor, knowing you can return whenever you like, and knowing that the person you have just met will always be there for you. You open the door and walk through to the other side, where someone else who loves you very much is sitting beside you — right now. You feel safe, warm and relaxed."

Index of Values and Issues

These two complementary indexes cover the specific topics that the 20 stories of this book are designed to address directly or by implication. The same topics are covered from two different perspectives: positive (Values) and negative (Issues). Each index reference consists of an abbreviated story title, followed by the page number on which the story begins.

141

ISSUES

Acknowledgments

The Publishers and Story Editor would like to thank their three
principal storytellers for writing the stories listed below:

Joyce Dunbar: Angela's Toyshop,
The Clown in the Sky,
The Weather Dance, The Circus
of Dreams, The River Moves On

Kate Petty: As Gentle as an
Elephant, The Snow Rabbit,
Treasure under the Sea,
The Fireside Cat, An Ancient
Oak Tree, Peter's Last Voyage,
A Blackbird Sings, Like a Firefly

Louisa Somerville: Dancing
with Butterflies, The Statue in
the Park, The Magic Pebble,
The Joyful Jungle